BABY TURKEYS

by Martha London

Jefferson Twp. Public Library
1031 Weldon Road
Oak Ridge, NJ 07438
973-208-6244
www.jeffersonlibrary.net

Cody Koala

An Imprint of Pop!
popbooksonline.com

abdobooks.com
Published by Pop!, a division of ABDO, PO Box 398166, Minneapolis,
Minnesota 55439. Copyright © 2021 by POP, LLC. International copyrights
reserved in all countries. No part of this book may be reproduced in any
form without written permission from the publisher. Pop!™ is a trademark
and logo of POP, LLC.

Printed in the United States of America, North Mankato, Minnesota

052020
092020

**THIS BOOK CONTAINS
RECYCLED MATERIALS**

Cover Photo: Maia Kennedy/Alamy
Interior Photos: Maia Kennedy/Alamy, 1; Shutterstock Images, 5 (top),
5 (bottom left), 5 (bottom right), 9, 10, 13 (top), 13 (bottom left), 13 (bottom
right), 14, 17, 18, 21; Larry Lefever/Grant Heilman Photography/Alamy, 6

Editor: Nick Rebman
Series Designer: Christine Ha

Library of Congress Control Number: 2019955137
Publisher's Cataloging-in-Publication Data
Names: London, Martha, author.
Title: Baby turkeys / by Martha London
Description: Minneapolis, Minnesota : POP!, 2021 | Series: Baby farm
    animals | Includes online resources and index
Identifiers: ISBN 9781532167492 (lib. bdg.) | ISBN 9781532168598 (ebook)
Subjects: LCSH: Turkeys--Juvenile literature. | Chicks--Juvenile literature. |
    Baby chicks--Juvenile literature. | Baby birds--Juvenile literature. | Baby
    farm animals--Juvenile literature. | Animal babies--Juvenile literature.
Classification: DDC 636.5/92--dc23

Hello! My name is

Cody Koala

Pop open this book and you'll find QR codes like this one, loaded with information, so you can learn even more!

Scan this code* and others like it while you read, or visit the website below to make this book pop.

popbooksonline.com/baby-turkeys

*Scanning QR codes requires a web-enabled smart device with a QR code reader app and a camera.

Table of Contents

Chapter 1

Warm and Dry

Turkeys are a type of bird. Baby turkeys are called **poults**. Farmers raise turkeys in large barns. Poults hatch from eggs.

A female turkey lays up to 12 eggs at one time.

Watch a video here!

Poults hatch in a **brooder house**. The young turkeys have soft, fluffy feathers. Poults stay in the brooder house for approximately eight weeks. The house keeps them warm and dry.

Chapter 2

Mealtime

Farmers give baby turkeys food and water. Turkeys eat vegetables and insects. They also eat **pellets**. The pellets are made of corn and soybeans.

Learn more here!

Turkeys have beaks. But they do not have teeth. They cannot chew the pellets. Instead, turkeys also eat small stones. These stones are called grit. They grind up the food in the turkey's stomach.

Chapter 3

Growing Up

Baby turkeys lose their soft feathers when they are two months old. They grow their adult feathers. These feathers are heavier. They keep turkeys warm and dry.

Complete an activity here!

Domestic turkeys grow quickly. They gain 1 pound (0.5 kg) every two weeks. Turkeys are fully grown when they are six months old. Farmers can keep or sell turkeys at that time.

Male turkeys gobble. Female turkeys cluck.

Chapter 4

Raising Turkeys

Many farmers raise turkeys for meat. Farmers sell the turkeys when they are fully grown. But people raise turkeys for more than just meat.

Learn more here!

For example, turkey feathers can go in pillows. Turkey feathers also have lots of **protein** in them. Some people grind the feathers and add them to animal **feed**.

Each turkey has approximately 3,500 feathers.

Farmers do not sell all of their turkeys. They keep some at the farm. In the spring, female turkeys **breed** with male turkeys. Farmers make sure the eggs hatch. Then they raise the new **poults**.

Making Connections

Text-to-Self

Would you want to see a baby turkey on a farm?
Why or why not?

Text-to-Text

Have you read books about other farm animals?
How are turkeys similar to and different from those
animals?

Text-to-World

How might the world be different if people did not
raise turkeys?

Glossary

breed – to make babies.

brooder house – a place that keeps baby birds safe and warm.

domestic – raised by humans, not in the wild.

feed – food that is given to an animal.

pellet – a small, hard piece of food for turkeys.

poult – a baby turkey.

protein – a healthy substance found in meat, eggs, and beans, which gives humans and animals energy.

Index

Online Resources

popbooksonline.com

Thanks for reading this Cody Koala book!

Scan this code* and others like it in this book, or visit the website below to make this book pop!

popbooksonline.com/baby-turkeys

*Scanning QR codes requires a web-enabled smart device with a QR code reader app and a camera.